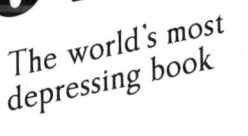

THE COLOURING BOOK FOR GOTHS

The world's most depressing book

D1407132

FOR
THE ANTICHRIST

(my girlfriend)

Tom Devonald is a UK-based
writer and graphic designer.

Known to friends for his love of doodling and his
terrible memory. His main topics of interest are
psychology, design, philosophy and psychology.

domtevonald.com

THIS IS A CARLTON BOOK

Published by Carlton Books Ltd
20 Mortimer Street
London WIT 3JW

A CIP catalogue record for this book is available from the British Library

10 9 8 7 6 5 4 3 2 1

ISBN 978-1-78097-810-9

Printed in China

THE COLOURING BOOK FOR GOTHS

The world's most depressing book

Tom Devonald

CARLTON BOOKS

Some of us understand that
there is wonder in woe,
mystery in the macabre
and light in the darkness.

PUTTING THE "FUN" IN "FUNERAL"

Colouring books are the new black

They are reported to have therapeutic effects that are good for your mental state.

It's even been claimed that they alleviate the symptoms of depression...

But what if you like being depressed?

What if you enjoy feeling off colour?

Whether you want to be melancholy or mirthless, morose or moody, this book allows you to enjoy all the fun of the new zeitgeist without conforming to the mainstream or running the risk of accidentally acquiring a sunny disposition.

BLACK
TO THE
DRAWING
BOARD

USE WHATEVER
TOOL YOU LIKE;
JUST MAKE SURE IT'S
B L A C K

INSTRUCTIONS

To cultivate and maintain a bleak outlook or simply to heighten a pre-existing demeanour of aloof cynicism, follow steps 1 and 2:

STEP 1

Fill out the following sheets IN BLACK, taking care to be neat and not colour outside the pages.

STEP 2

Sit back and marvel at your mastery of the miserable.

PRACTICE PAGE

Fill in this "colour by numbers"
page for a bit of a warm-up.

1 = Jet black
2= Pitch black
3= Ebony

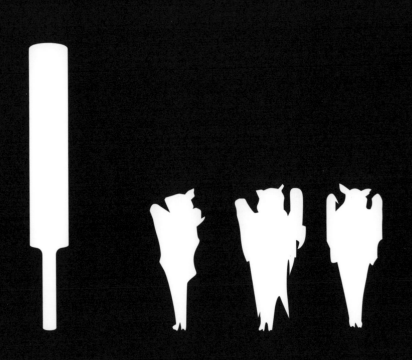

BLINDNESS

A DARK NIGHT

A DARK KNIGHT

A DARK HORSE

BLACK BEAUTY

A MELANISTIC UNICORN

A ZEBRA SEEN THROUGH THE BARS AT THE ZOO

BEING STUCK AT THE BOTTOM OF A VERY DEEP WELL
(AT NIGHT)

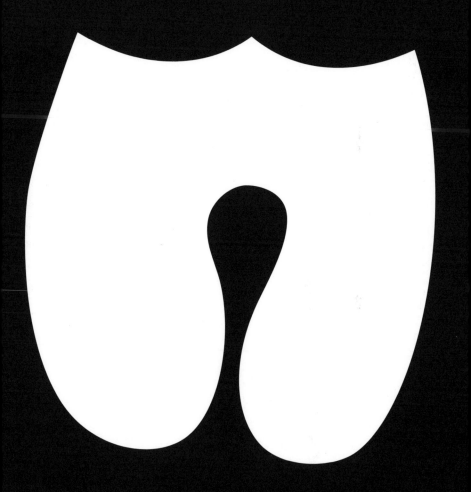

THE LAST THING THAT BAT SAW
WHEN OZZY BIT ITS HEAD OFF

THE HORRIFYING UNSPEAKABLE TRUTH
THAT UNDERLIES REALITY

A NINJA WITH TWO BLACK EYES
(IN STEALTH MODE)

WOOD

GLOOM

NOTHING

NOTHINGNESS

YIN AND YIN

A SQUID ATTACK TO THE FACE

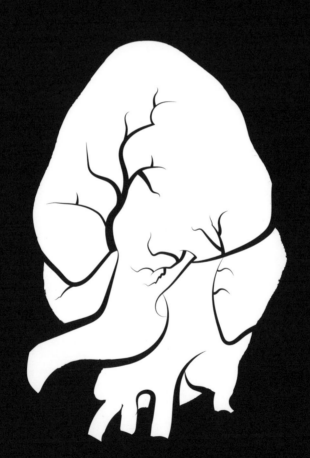

YOUR EX'S HEART

A SEA GULL
(IN AN OIL SLICK)

A CROW

A MAGPIE
(IN A LITTLE LEATHER JACKET)

A BLACKBIRD

THE DARK SIDE OF THE MOON

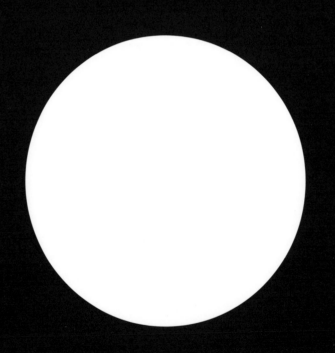

A REALLY DARK ECLIPSE

THE INEVITABLE

A BADGER IN A BALAKLAVA

LOOKING UP AT THE NIGHT SKY
(IN A HEAVILY POLLUTED CITY)

THE BUTTOCKS OF A BURLESQUE
DANCER IN SKIN-TIGHT PVC,
(VIEWED THROUGH THE BINOCULARS
OF A DISTANT PERVERT)

A POWER CUT

A DUNGEON
(DURING A POWER CUT)

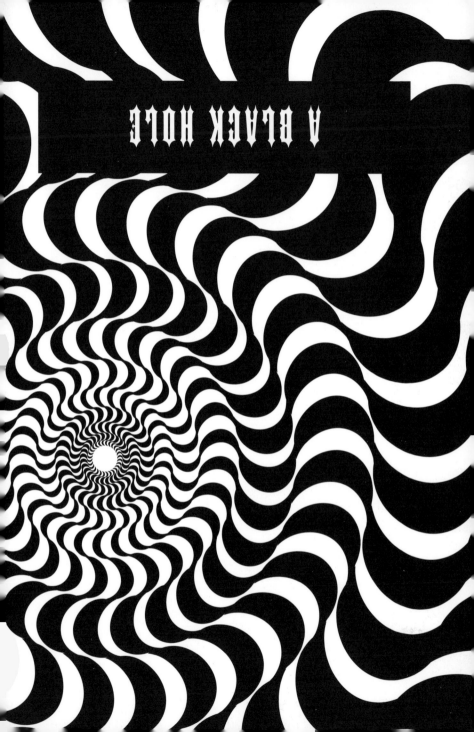

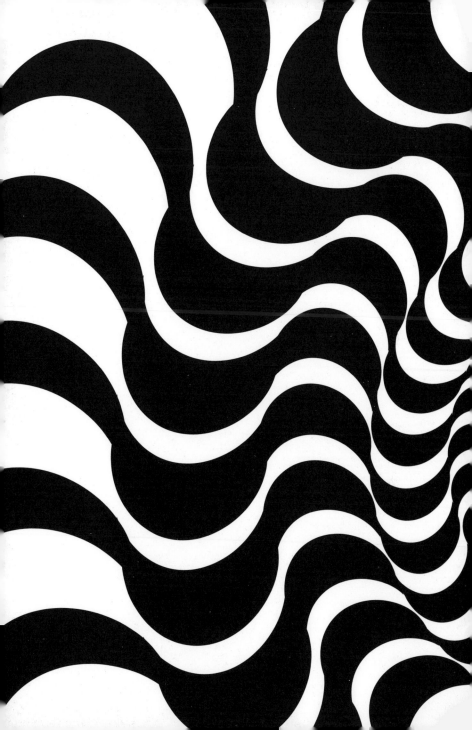

THE ABYSS

A PANDA IN WITNESS PROTECTION
(DISGUISED AS A BLACK BEAR)

YOUR SOUL

NIHILISM

THE MAJESTIC POLAR BEAR
(IN MIDWINTER AT THE NORTH POLE)

SOMETHING LURKING IN THE DARK

AN INSECURE KILLER WHALE

WEARING TOO MUCH EYE SHADOW

WAKING UP INSIDE A COFFIN

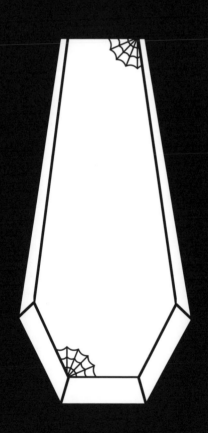

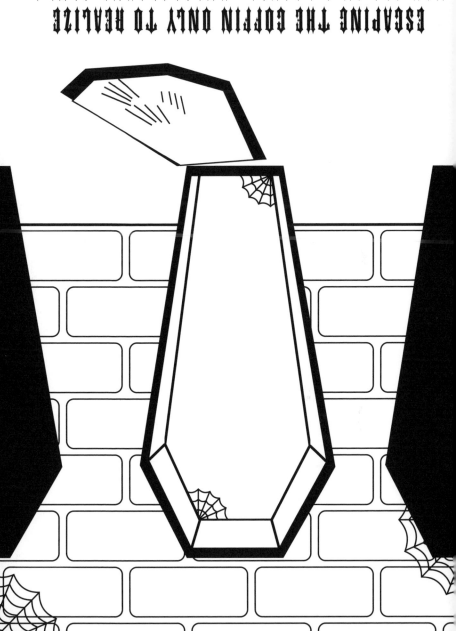

ESCAPING THE COFFIN ONLY TO REALIZE
YOU ARE IN A LOCKED, UNDERGROUND CRYPT

YESTERDAY

TOMORROW

BLACKING OUT FROM TERROR

A BLACK CAT
CROSSING YOUR PATH

THE BEST SEX YOU EVER HAD
(WHILE BLINDFOLDED)

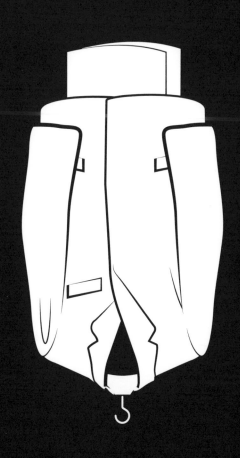

JOHNNY CASH'S
DRY CLEANING

EXIT LIGHT

ENTER NIGHT

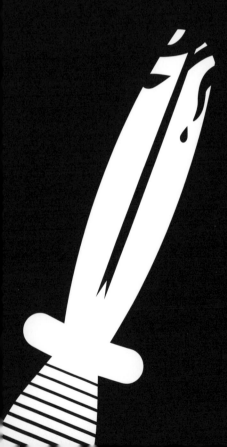

SLEEP

A PANTHER MAULING
A TERRORIST

AN INVISIBLE MAN LYING DOWN IN A ROAD

A TRUCK WITH NO HEADLIGHTS

THE REMAINS OF AN
INVISIBLE MAN
(STREWN ACROSS A ROAD)

A RABBIT IN A HAT
(AN AIRTIGHT HAT)

A SHADOW

A RED DOOR
(AFTER MICK JAGGER HAS BEEN AT IT)

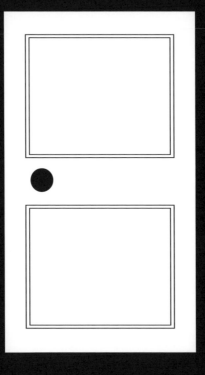

THE ABSENCE OF COLOUR

INTROSPECTION

A MAN DROWNING
IN A TAR PIT

KETTLE

THE UNKNOWN

THE UNKNOWABLE

NIETZSCHE'S MOUSTACHE

THE FLEETING MOMENT WHEN YOU BLINK

YOUR DARK SIDE

YOUR OTHER SIDE

DARTH VADER
LOOKING FOR A LIGHT SWITCH

OBLIVION

HAD ENOUGH OF COLOURING IN?

... GET READY FOR THE

"FUN"

SECTION

CULT CUTS

How many of these gothic style-setters can you recognize just by their hair-do?

IT'S A COVER UP!

Help these proto-goths leave the past behind them by covering up their embarrassing ink with new tattoos.

The unsuccessful
"if-i-get-a-tattoo-she-can-never-leave-m[...]
tatto[...]

The unintentionally phallic tribal tatoo

轻信

The Chinese symbol for "Gulli[...]

#NOPE

The sociopathic "pop-culture-forehead" tattoo

Fat profits

The "double-whammy" tattoo

Hanson

The "regrettable-band-name" tattoo

Smoke Crouich

The misspelled "weed-is-my-identity" tattoo

MAZE

Can you help Sammy
the skeleton and Dave
the ghost escape their
underground crypts?

BALLS

1 2 3 4 5 6 7 8 9 10 11 12 13 14 15

JOIN THE DOTS

GOOD · EVIL

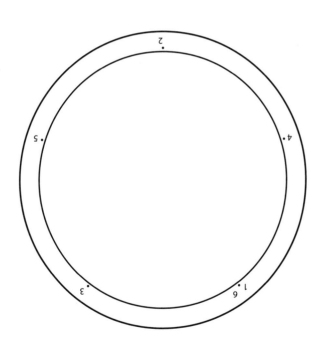

INVERTED-CROSSWORD

ACROSS

1: An anagram of "tish"

2: The opposite of "isn't"

DOWN

3: A competitor who
   scores no points.

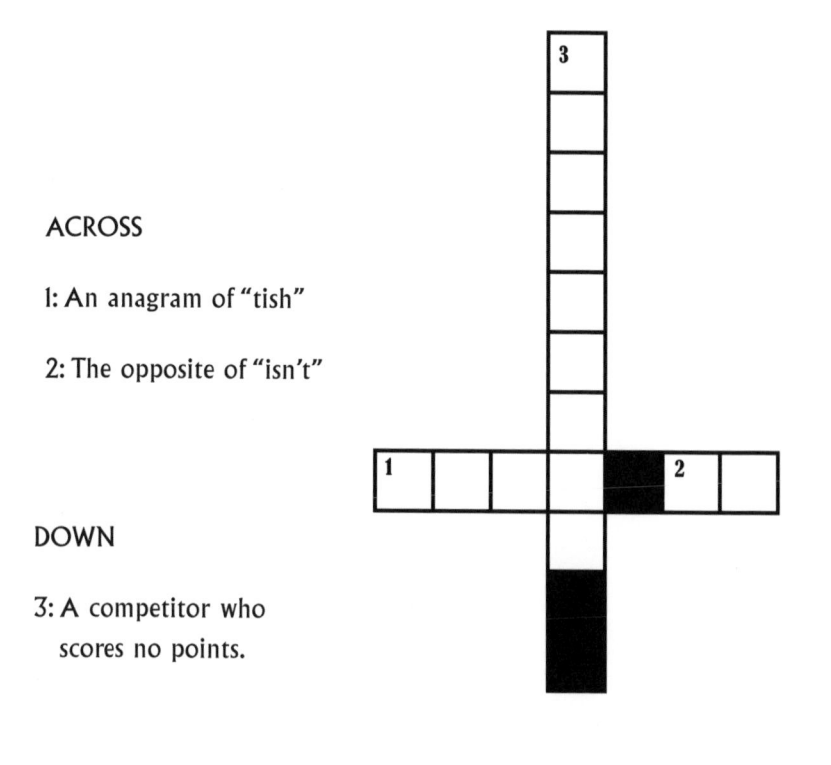

WORD SEARCH

"Play" this record backwards
(starting at the centre)
to reveal 3 hidden messages.

INNOCENT-HANGMAN

Find a friend (or an enemy) to play these
extreme versions of Hangman with.

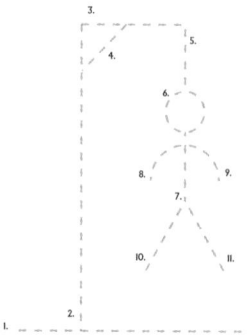

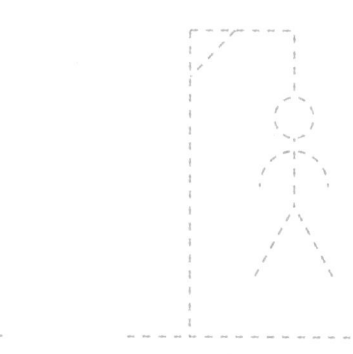

(This guy is genuinely innocent)

(This guy only confessed to save his brother)

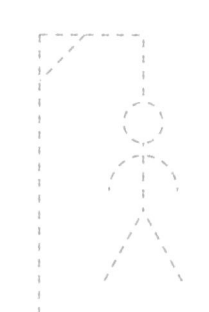

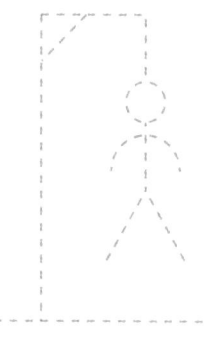

(The guy this guy killed was a complete asshole,
he honestly did us all a favour)

(This guy's twin did it)

HIGH-STAKES HANGMAN

These men are hanging on your every word.

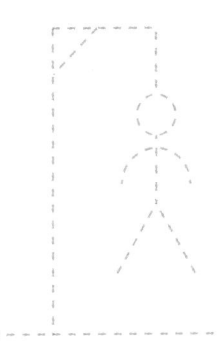

(This guy is on the verge of curing cancer)

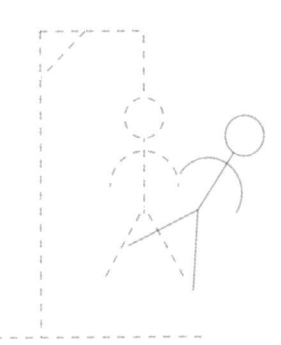

(This guy's siamese twin will die as well)

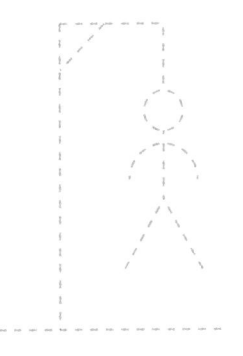

(This is your mum)

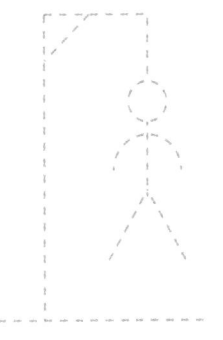

(This guy owes you money)

GOTH HAIRCUTS QUIZ

A: Robert Smith

B: Morticia Addams

C: Kat Von D

D: Dita Von Teese

E: That forensics girl off of CSI

F: Edgar Allen Poe (Goth ground zero)

G: Gary Numan

H: Marilyn Manson

I: Wednesday Addams

MAZE-BALLS

Sammy the skeleton: There is no solution; trying is the problem.

Dave the Ghost: Ghosts can go through walls, idiot.

INVERTED CROSSWORD

1: "This"

2: "IS"

3: "Pointless"

WORD SEARCH

Hidden messages:

"Hail the Dark Lord"

"Evil will prevail"

"Eat gluten"

P.S.

Did you spot the hidden ghoulies in the intro pages?

You did? Ten points to Slytherin!

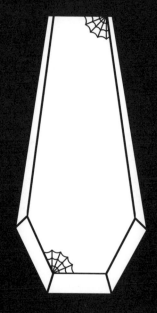

...SOLUTIONS

HANG YOUR MASTERPIECES ON
TWITTER, INSTAGRAM OR FACEBOOK
WITH THE HASHTAG

#TCBFG

AND YOU MIGHT JUST WIN
SOME ORIGINAL ART!

DRAWN
THEN
HUNG

FANGS FOR READING...

Now that you're feeling suitably miserable why not upload a picture of yourself (AKA a "Hellfie") so you can savour the suffering?

#TCBFG

(back cover)